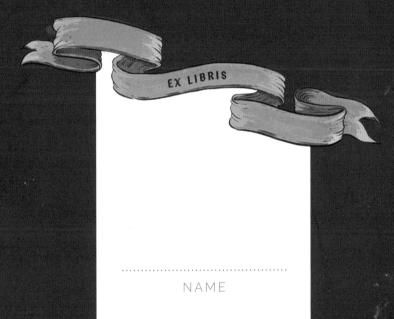

EX LIBRIS

NAME

ACROSTIC THEOLOGY FOR KIDS SERIES

Book 1

The Acrostic of God

·

Book 2

The Acrostic of Jesus

·

Book 3

The Acrostic of Salvation

·

Book 4

The Acrostic of Scripture

A RHYMING BIBLICAL THEOLOGY FOR KIDS

THE
ACROSTIC
OF
SCRIPTURE

JONATHAN GIBSON & TIMOTHY BRINDLE

ILLUSTRATED BY
C. S. FRITZ

New Growth Press

New Growth Press, Greensboro, NC 27401
Text Copyright © 2023 by Jonathan Gibson and Timothy Brindle
Illustration Copyright © 2023 by C. S. Fritz

Cover/Interior Design and Typesetting: Trish Mahoney, themahoney.com
Cover/Interior illustrations: C. S. Fritz
Art typeset in Cinder by Fort Foundry

ISBN: 978-1-64507-337-6
Library of Congress Control Number: 2022944536

Printed in India

30 29 28 27 26 25 24 23   1 2 3 4 5

The Acrostic Theology for Kids Series

"And these words that I command you today shall be on your heart. You shall teach them diligently to your children, and shall talk of them when you sit in your house, and when you walk by the way, and when you lie down, and when you rise." Deuteronomy 6:6–7

The inspiration behind these acrostic books comes from John Calvin, the Genevan Reformer. In 1542, Calvin simplified his Catechism for the Genevan Church (1537) so that children could better understand and memorize the essential truths of the Christian Faith. It was entitled *The French ABCs*.

These acrostic books are not strictly catechetical (questions and answers), but they are written in that same tradition of instruction. As such, they are a means of planting the good seed of God's Word into the hearts of children, so that they might grow in the grace and knowledge of the Lord Jesus. We hope the new element of an acrostic poem set to rhyme may help the truths about God (theology), Jesus (Christology), salvation (soteriology), and Scripture (Biblical theology) to stick a little bit better. The books may be read in one sitting (either by parent/teacher or child) or they may be used for family devotions, taking one letter per day for families to meditate on, with some accompanying Bible verses.

We are praying that this series will be used by the Spirit to allow children and parents to grow in the knowledge of God and thus to love and trust him more. Enjoy!

Jonny Gibson and Timothy Brindle

See back of book for more information about how to use this book with children. Use the QR code to hear Timothy Brindle read aloud *The Acrostic of Scripture* in rap style. To purchase *The Acrostic of Scripture* music album, visit www.timothybrindleministries.com.

Dedication

For Noah, Ellie, and Phoebe; Malachi and Abigail

"Open my eyes,
that I may behold wondrous
things out of your law."
Psalm 119:18

PROLOGUE

Let's read the Acrostic of *Scripture together*
So our knowledge of God's big *picture is better*.
We'll read it, rap it, *sing it—it's fun*!
Till Jesus comes back and his *kingdom has come*.

An acrostic poem uses the *alphabet*
To teach you God's truth, so you will *not forget*.
God does this in Scripture, like Psalm *One Nineteen*;
In Lamentations, he has a *fun rhyme scheme*.
So, from now on, we'll use the *first letter*
To help us to learn the Lord's *Word better*.
He's the Alpha and Omega; yes, from *A to Z*;
From Genesis to Revelation, it's *plain to see*.
Each page has a person, place, or event from the *Bible*
To show it's one big story leading to Christ's *arrival*.
He says, "In all your ways, *acknowledge me*";
Kids, let's learn biblical *theology*!
What's biblical theology? It's the *study of Scripture*,
That shows how all the stories point to Christ—
　　the *wonderful victor*.
Not just to see how Scripture *connects together*,
But to see God's Word as our *precious treasure*.

Let's read the Acrostic of *Scripture together*
So our knowledge of the big *picture is better*.
We'll read it, rap it, *sing it—it's fun*!
Till Jesus comes back and his *kingdom has come*.

Adam

Adam was created by God as the *first human;*

His sin brought us all into the *worst ruin.*

What he did counts for us—by his *works we are cursed;*

But in Christ, the Last Adam, the *curse is reversed.*

....

Romans 5:19 For as by the one man's disobedience the many were made sinners, so by the one man's obedience the many will be made righteous.

Babel

Babel—the city where man makes a name for his *own praise;*

And even tries to make it to heaven by his *own ways.*

So God changed their languages—throughout the earth
they're *scattered—*

But he promised through Abraham's son they would be
gathered.

....

Genesis 11:9 Therefore its name was called Babel, because there
the Lord confused the language of all the earth. And from there
the Lord dispersed them over the face of all the earth.

Genesis 12:3 "I will bless those who bless you, and him who
dishonors you I will curse, **and in you all the tribes of the earth shall
be blessed."** (AT)

Revelation 7:9–10 After this I looked, and behold, **a great multitude
that no one could number, from every nation, from all tribes and
peoples and languages, standing before the throne and before the
Lamb,** clothed in white robes, with palm branches in their hands,
and crying out with a loud voice, "Salvation belongs to our God who
sits on the throne, and to the Lamb!"

Covenant

Covenant—a special promise God *makes with us*,

In which he requires us to *obey and trust*.

The LORD God first made with Adam a *covenant of works*:

Life if he obeyed; but if he sinned—*judgment was the curse*.

So God made another one—a *covenant of grace*;

His Son would come to take the *judgment in our place*.

This covenant with Abraham, Israel, and *David*

Is faithfully fulfilled in Jesus, just as he *stated*.

....

Matthew 26:27–28 And he took a cup, and when he had given thanks he gave it to them, saying, "Drink of it, all of you, **for this is my blood of the covenant, which is poured out for many for the forgiveness of sins**."

2 Corinthians 1:20 For all the promises of God find their Yes in him. That is why it is through him that we utter our Amen to God for his glory.

DAVID

David—the shepherd king, a man after God's own *heart*;

He wrote psalms to praise the Lord, which he sung with his *harp*.

God promised him a son who would be *greater than him*;

Jesus was raised to reign after *he paid for our sin*.

....

1 Samuel 13:14 The LORD has sought out a man after his own heart, and the LORD has commanded him to be prince over his people, because you have not kept what the LORD commanded you.

2 Samuel 7:12–13 When your days are fulfilled and you lie down with your fathers, I will raise up your offspring after you, who shall come from your body, and I will establish his kingdom. He shall build a house for my name, and I will establish the throne of his kingdom forever.

Eden

Eden is the garden where God placed *Adam and Eve*;

But then came the serpent and they were *badly deceived*.

In Adam we're disqualified to eat from the *tree of life*;

But we'll live forever in the New Eden as *Jesus's wife*.

....

Genesis 2:15 **Then the Lord God took the man and he placed him in the garden of Eden** in order to serve it and to guard it. (AT)

Revelation 19:6–8 Then I heard what seemed to be the voice of a great multitude, like the roar of many waters and like the sound of mighty peals of thunder, crying out, "Hallelujah! For the Lord our God the Almighty reigns. Let us rejoice and exult and give him the glory, **for the marriage of the Lamb has come, and his Bride has made herself ready**; it was granted her to clothe herself with fine linen, bright and pure"—for the fine linen is the righteous deeds of the saints.

Closing Refrain

Now we've read the Acrostic of *Scripture together*;

Let's study his Word so that we *live for him better*.

Pray: "Lord, help us love your Word, so we're *treasuring your glory*;

Open our eyes to see Christ is the *center of the story*."

Zacchaeus

Zacchaeus—he was a sinful little *tax collector*,

Till he met him who could heal the blind and cleanse a
  ghastly leper.

Jesus came to his house, changed his heart, and forgave
  all his sin;

He will do the same for you if you repent and *call on him*!

....

Luke 19:8–10 And **Zacchaeus** stood and said to the Lord, **"Behold,
Lord, the half of my goods I give to the poor. And if I have defrauded
anyone of anything, I restore it fourfold."** And Jesus said to him,
"Today salvation has come to this house, since he also is a son of
Abraham. For the Son of Man came to seek and to save the lost."

Yahweh

Yahweh—God's Hebrew name, which he says we *have
to remember*;
Written as "Lᴏʀᴅ" in your Bible with each *capital letter*.
It stands for "Yahweh" and his promise to *be with his people*;
The "I AM" became a man to *redeem them from evil*.

. . . .

Exodus 3:12–15 — [God] said, "**But I will be with you** . . ." Then Moses
said to God, "If I come to the people of Israel and say to them, 'The
God of your fathers has sent me to you,' and they ask me, 'What is
his name?' what shall I say to them?" God said to Moses, "**I ᴀᴍ ᴡʜᴏ I
ᴀᴍ.**" And he said, "Say this to the people of Israel: '**I ᴀᴍ has sent me
to you.**'" God also said to Moses, "Say this to the people of Israel: '**The
Lᴏʀᴅ, the God of your fathers, the God of Abraham, the God of Isaac,
and the God of Jacob, has sent me to you.' This is my name forever,
and thus I am to be remembered throughout all generations.**"

eXodus

eXodus—the LORD rescued Israel from *Egypt*:

"I have heard your cries; and your suffering, I've *seen it*."

The Lord God brought his people through the Red Sea on
dry *ground*;

Like the flood, he judged Egyptians with water, and they
drowned.

. . . .

Exodus 14:27–29 **And as the Egyptians fled into it, the LORD threw
the Egyptians into the midst of the sea.** The waters returned and
covered the chariots and the horsemen; **of all the host of Pharaoh
that had followed them into the sea, not one of them remained.**
But the people of Israel walked on dry ground through the sea, the
waters being a wall to them on their right hand and on their left.

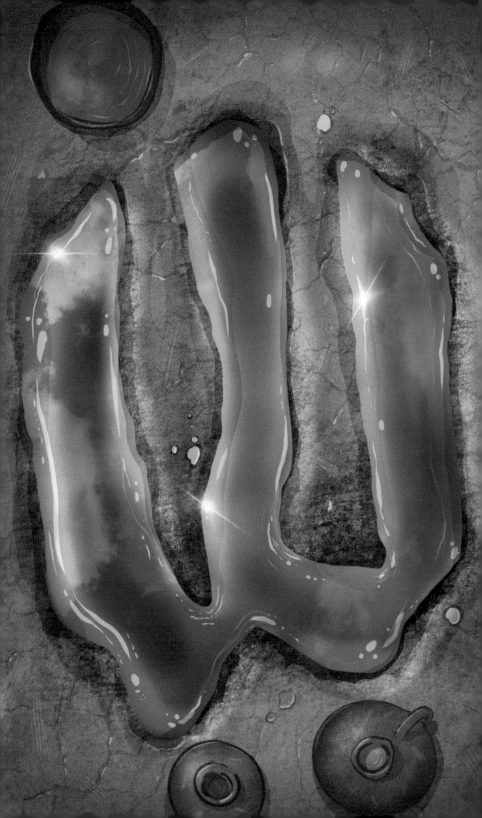

WELL

Well of water—where God provides wives in the *Torah*
we notice:
Rebekah for Isaac, Rachel for Jacob, *Zipporah for Moses*.
It was where Jesus met the woman who was a *Samaritan*;
He said he gives the living water, so we'll never *thirst again*.

....

John 4:13–14 Jesus said to her, "Everyone who drinks of this water
will be thirsty again, **but whoever drinks of the water that I will give
him will never be thirsty again. The water that I will give him will
become in him a spring of water welling up to eternal life."**

VEIL

Veil—back in the Old Testament, this was the *temple curtain*,
To separate a holy God from every *sinful person*.
It kept sinners from going into the *Most Holy Place*;
But it was torn when Christ died—for us to *behold his face*.

....

Mark 15:37–38 But Jesus let out a loud cry, and died. **And the veil of the temple was torn in two from top to bottom.** (NASB)

Hebrews 10:19–22 Therefore, brothers and sisters, **since we have confidence to enter the holy place by the blood of Jesus, by a new and living way which He inaugurated for us through the veil, that is, through His flesh,** and since we have a great priest over the house of God, let's approach God with a sincere heart in full assurance of faith, having our hearts sprinkled clean from an evil conscience and our bodies washed with pure water. (NASB)

UZZAH

Uzzah reached out and touched the ark of the *covenant*,

So the Lord struck him down dead as a just *punishment*.

Only Levites could carry it; they used *poles on its side*;

What became of Uzzah? Since God is *holy, he died*.

. . . .

2 Samuel 6:6–7 And when they came to the threshing floor of Nacon, Uzzah put out his hand to the ark of God and took hold of it, for the oxen stumbled. And the anger of the LORD was kindled against Uzzah, and God struck him down there because of his error, and he died there beside the ark of God.

Temple

Temple—is the house of God where he *dwells with his people;*

Because he's holy, he must *expel all that's evil.*

Eden was his earthly temple, but Adam's sin made him *wrathful;*

Then God dwelt with Israel by his grace in the *tabernacle.*

In Jerusalem, when King Solomon built the *temple building,*

His glory appeared—like when the tabernacle *tent was filling.*

Christ called himself the temple, since he shares his Father's *essence;*

The church is now his temple, until in his heavenly *presence.*

. . . .

Revelation 21:3, 22 And I heard a loud voice from the throne saying, "Behold, the tabernacle of God is with man. He will dwell with them, and they will be his people, and God himself will be with them as their God. . . . **And I saw no temple in the city, for its temple is the Lord God the Almighty and the Lamb.**" (AT)

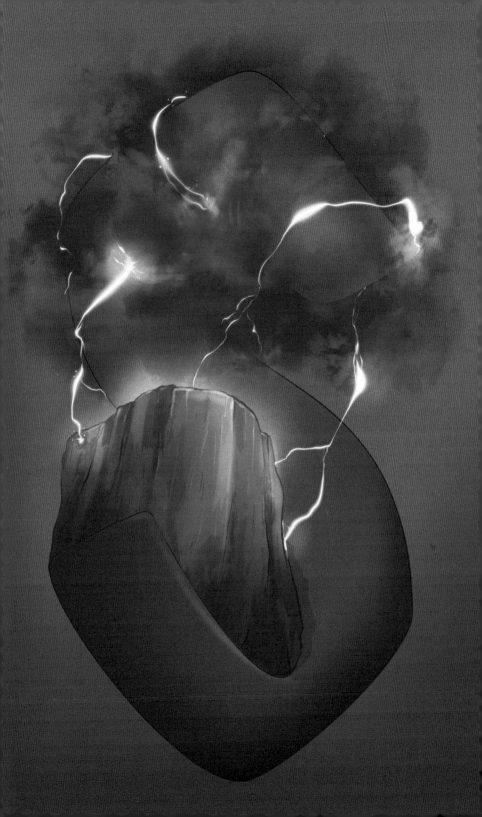

Sinai

Sinai—the mountain where the Lord came *down to give*
    his Law;
Fire and cloud surrounded it, *astoundingly in awe.*
God's standard of holiness is still the *Ten Commandments;*
Christ obeyed them perfectly, then died for *sinful bandits.*

....

Exodus 19:18–20 **Now Mount Sinai was wrapped in smoke because
the Lord had descended on it in fire.** The smoke of it went up like
the smoke of a kiln, and the whole mountain trembled greatly. And
as the sound of the trumpet grew louder and louder, Moses spoke,
and God answered him in thunder. **The Lord came down on Mount
Sinai, to the top of the mountain.** And the Lord called Moses to the
top of the mountain, and Moses went up.

Ruth

Ruth—this Gentile woman married the son of *Naomi*;

When their husbands died in Moab, Ruth served the true

God *only*.

Then Boaz took Ruth the Moabite to be his own *wife*,

And she became the "great-grandmother" of the King of *life*.

....

Ruth 4:13, 17 — **So Boaz took Ruth, and she became his wife. And he went in to her, and the Lord gave her conception, and she bore a son**. . . . And the women of the neighborhood gave him a name, saying, "A son has been born to Naomi." **They named him Obed. He was the father of Jesse, the father of David.**

Queen Esther

Queen Esther—she was raised by her uncle *Mordecai*;

She pleaded to the king for the Jews before they *were to die*.

The king listened to her request—because it was God's
    sovereign plan,

To preserve his people and return them to the *Promised Land*.

. . . .

Esther 4:14 For if you keep silent at this time, **relief and deliverance will rise for the Jews from another place,** but you and your father's house will perish. **And who knows whether you have not come to the kingdom for such a time as this?**

Pentecost

Pentecost—the Spirit was poured out on Christ's *church and brethren*;

After Christ died, he was buried, then raised, and *returned to heaven*.

The Holy Spirit empowered the preaching of *Peter and Paul*;

You'll receive the Spirit, if upon the name of *Jesus you call*!

. . . .

Acts 2:1–2, 4, 14, 16–17, 21 When the day of **Pentecost** arrived, they were all together in one place. And suddenly there came from heaven a sound like a mighty rushing wind, and it filled the entire house where they were sitting. . . . And **they were all filled with the Holy Spirit** and began to speak in other tongues as the Spirit gave them utterance. . . . **Peter** . . . **lifted up his voice and addressed them**: . . . "But this is what was uttered through the prophet Joel: 'And in the last days it shall be, God declares, that I will pour out my Spirit on all flesh . . . And it shall come to pass that **everyone who calls upon the name of the Lord shall be saved.'"**

Offspring

Offspring of the woman, promised to destroy the *serpent*;
He is also the offspring of Abraham, God's *servant*.
Is this the same offspring who's promised to David?
    That's true!
We can tell that it's Jesus from the first verse in *Matthew*!
On David's throne he sits, his blessing is for all *nations*—
Africans, Europeans, Americans, and *Asians*.
Jesus saves people from every language, *nation, and clan*;
By faith in Christ, we are also offspring of *Abraham*!

....

Genesis 3:15 I will put enmity between you and the woman, and between your offspring and her offspring; **he shall crush your head, although you shall crush his heel.** (AT)

Matthew 1:1 The book of the genealogy of **Jesus Christ, the son of David, the son of Abraham.**

Galatians 3:16, 29 Now the promises were made to Abraham and to his offspring. It does not say, "And to offsprings," referring to many, **but referring to one, "And to your offspring," who is Christ.** . . . And if you are Christ's, then you are Abraham's offspring, heirs according to promise.

Nehemiah and New Jerusalem

Nehemiah—the man God enabled to *rebuild the city*

Of Jerusalem, because the Lord God was *filled with pity*.

But the New Jerusalem is greater—there's no *comparing*;

It is the Heavenly City that Jesus is *preparing*.

....

Nehemiah 2:4–5 Then the king said to me, "What are you requesting?" So I prayed to the God of heaven. And I said to the king, **"If it pleases the king, and if your servant has found favor in your sight, that you send me to Judah, to the city of my fathers' graves, that I may rebuild it."**

John 14:3 **And if I go and prepare a place for you,** I will come again and will take you to myself, that where I am you may be also.

Moses

Moses led God's people out of Egyptian *slavery*;

Then received the law and saw God's glory *amazingly*.

God promised another prophet would come just like *Moses*;

It is Jesus! And Peter's sermon in Acts three *shows this*.

. . . .

Deuteronomy 18:15 **The Lord your God will raise up for you a prophet like me from among you, from your brothers**—it is to him you shall listen.

Acts 3:18, 22 But what God foretold by the mouth of all the prophets, that his Christ would suffer, he thus fulfilled. . . . **Moses said, "The Lord God will raise up for you a prophet like me from your brothers. You shall listen to him in whatever he tells you."**

LEVITICUS

Leviticus—written as God's holiness *manual*;

It's about how priests are to sacrifice an *animal*.

Jesus came as the final priest and final *sacrifice*;

On the cross God the Father poured out all his *wrath on Christ*.

....

Leviticus 16:15 Then [Aaron the high priest] shall kill the goat of the sin offering that is for the people and bring its blood inside the veil and do with its blood as he did with the blood of the bull, sprinkling it over the mercy seat and in front of the mercy seat.

Hebrews 9:11–12 But when Christ appeared as a high priest of the good things that have come, then through the greater and more perfect tent (not made with hands, that is, not of this creation) he entered once for all into the holy places, not by means of the blood of goats and calves but by means of his own blood, thus securing an eternal redemption.

Kingdom of God

Kingdom of God is the big story of *Scripture*;

Adam failed to rule over Satan the *trickster*.

King David and Solomon couldn't beat sin or *Satan*;

But Christ did, ushering in God's kingdom of *salvation*.

. . . .

Colossians 1:13–14 He has delivered us from the domain of darkness **and transferred us to the kingdom of his beloved Son, in whom we have redemption**, the forgiveness of sins.

Joshua and Jesus

Joshua led God's people into the *Promised Land*;
God gave victory o'er the foe by his *sovereign hand*.
Greater than Joshua, Christ's word is *sharper than a sword*;
Jesus Christ is the Captain of the *Army of the Lord*!

· ·

Joshua 5:14 "I am the captain of the army of the Lord. Now I have
come." And Joshua fell on his face to the earth and worshiped. (AT)

Luke 23:42–43 And [the thief] said, "Jesus, remember me when
you come into your kingdom." And he said to him, "Truly, I say to
you, **today you will be with me in paradise."**

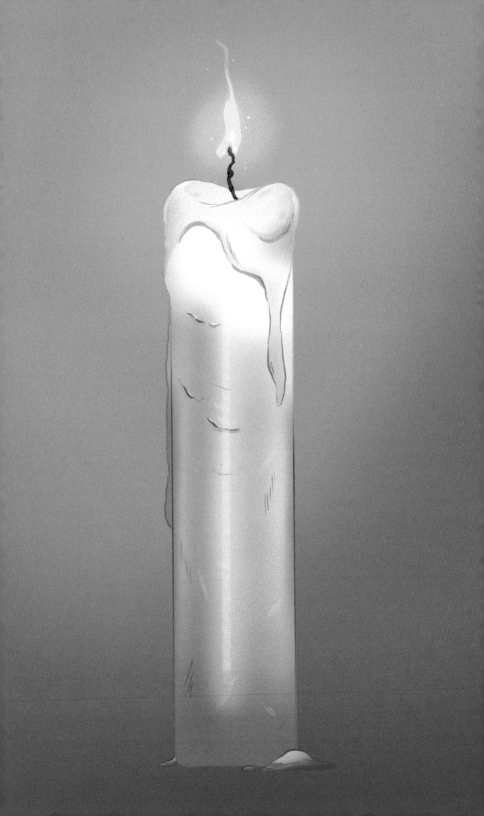

ISRAEL

Israel—the new name that God *gave to Jacob*;

A "holy nation" to praise God's *Name that's sacred*,

To serve the Lord alone as his *"kingdom of priests,"*

To worship him with psalms that they'd *sing at their feasts*.

When Matthew quotes Hosea eleven verse *one*,

He means that Jesus is God's true Israel *son*!

He's the "Light to Gentiles"—his *word provides the spark*;

You're a true Jew too if he's *circumcised your heart*.

Exodus 19:5–6 "Now therefore, if you will indeed obey my voice and keep my covenant, you shall be my treasured possession among all peoples, for all the earth is mine; **and you shall be to me a kingdom of priests and a holy nation**."

Isaiah 49:3, 6 And he said to me, "**You are my servant, Israel**, in whom I will be glorified. . . . It is too light a thing that you should be my servant to raise up the tribes of Jacob and to bring back the preserved of Israel; **I will make you as a light for the nations**, that my salvation may reach to the end of the earth."

Hosea 11:1 **When Israel was a child, I loved him, and out of Egypt I called my son.**

Matthew 2:15 This was to fulfill what the Lord had spoken by the prophet, "**Out of Egypt I called my son.**"

Hannah

Hannah couldn't have children—she cried out in her *barrenness*;
God heard her prayers because she was humble without
   arrogance.
Her son Samuel was born because God gave *life to her womb*;
Like when Jesus humbled himself, God raised *Christ from the
   tomb*.

. . . .

1 Samuel 1:20 **And in due time Hannah conceived and bore a son,
and she called his name Samuel,** for she said, "I have asked for him
from the LORD."

Romans 1:1–4 Paul, a servant of Christ Jesus, called to be an
apostle, set apart for the gospel of God, which he promised
beforehand through his prophets in the holy Scriptures, **concerning
his Son,** who was descended from David according to the flesh and
was **declared to be the Son of God in power according to the Spirit
of holiness by his resurrection from the dead, Jesus Christ our Lord.**

GOLIATH

Goliath—the Philistine giant *who defied the Lord*;

So David cut off his head with *Goliath's giant sword*.

Before that, with a stone from his sling, David *struck him dead*;

Just like Jesus did to Satan when he *crushed his head*.

. . . .

1 Samuel 17:50–51 **So David prevailed over the Philistine with a sling and with a stone, and struck the Philistine and killed him.** There was no sword in the hand of David. Then David ran and stood over the Philistine **and took his sword and drew it out of its sheath and killed him and cut off his head with it.**

Genesis 3:15 I will put enmity between you and the woman, and between your offspring and her offspring; **he shall bruise your head, and you shall bruise his heel.**

FLOOD

Flood of water—God poured it out when *destroying the earth*,

Because all human hearts were filled with sin's *poison from birth*.

God was just to pour out his wrath on all *humanity*;

But he was gracious to save Noah and his *family*.

....

2 Peter 2:5 If he did not spare the ancient world, **but preserved Noah, a herald of righteousness, with seven others, when he brought a flood upon the world of the ungodly.**

Hebrews 11:7 **By faith Noah**, being warned by God concerning events as yet unseen, **in reverent fear constructed an ark for the saving of his household.** By this he condemned the world and became an heir of the righteousness that comes by faith.